Take a Trip to
Diverse City

written by
Shawna Ray

illustrated by Laurie A. Faust

Rhythm Ray Publishing
P.O. Box 696, Huger, SC 29450
Email: info@rhythmray.com
www.rhythmray.com

Diverse City. Reprinted B5 Special Edition with music CD, January 15, 2008
Rhythm Ray Inc., Publishing and Promoting Movement and Light

www.rhythmray.com

Printed in South Korea

Copyright © 2007

Take a Trip to Diverse City, Originally published by Winters Press
No part of this publication may be reproduced transmitted or stored
in any form or by any means without written permission from the author
or publisher except for brief excerpts by reviewers.

Library of Congress Control Number 2006939176
ISBN 978-0-9800176-0-1

Dedicated to Zachary and Jacob:
May you always appreciate your differences
and treasure your friendship.

- S

'Twas a gray kind of day
    outside in Same City.

The school bell rang;
    recess was beginning.

Jacob and Zac tried to join the ball game.
  But some kids told Jacob that he couldn't play.

For his skin was "brown" and theirs was "white,"
  Zac stood by his friend knowing that was not right.

"Why?" he thought, "should it matter at all?"
          Each child in the class had a difference he saw.

"They're tripp'n!" said Jacob, and Zachary agreed.
"A trip – hey, let's all go to Diverse City!"

Some kids were afraid and chose not to go,
    But adventure is fun and soon many followed.

"Good food," Zac said,
"is the first thing we need.
Let's walk down the street
and get something to eat."

At Same Café, the food can be dull.
By adding some spice it becomes flavorful.

The aroma is sweet, and the menu delights.
Everyone can find something they like.

Embrace all the tastes and the sounds and the smells.
New friends are welcome to dine and to tell

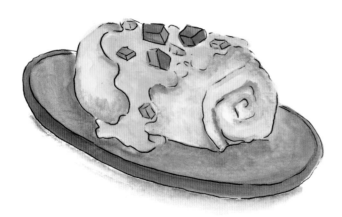

Stories and memories of journeys they've shared.
The table is open; acceptance is there.

Next stop is the art shop;
the colors are vast.
You can paint every shade,
be creative, and laugh.

Mold the soft clay into balls
and cool shapes.
Make a cup, a bowl, or
a tall flower vase.

We all have ideas that are new and exciting.
Let's color together or sit alone writing.

Think of a story,
    imagine the scene.
It's great to create
    when the mind is so free.

"Who wants to move on?" Zac said to his friends.
"I hear a cool sound that is drawing us in

To the streets where live music is filling the air;

A band plays aloud;
    music lifts like the moon,

Each different sound is forming a tune.

It then turns so gently
as the melodies change
To a ballad sung sweetly
like soft falling rain.

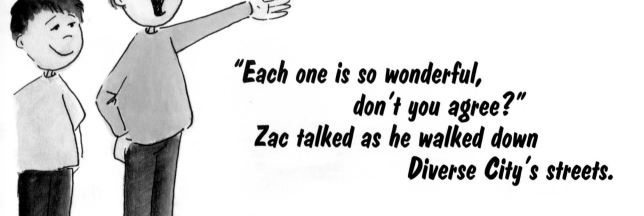

"Each one is so wonderful,
don't you agree?"
Zac talked as he walked down
Diverse City's streets.

There are people at work,
    each with skills of their own.
By joining together,
    we get much more done.

"If we all were the same, we'd be missing all this.
We need everyone to share their unique gift.

We learn from each other and life can be found
   In all styles and flavors, new sights and sounds."

As they returned to the classroom later that day,
The kids were different and everyone played.

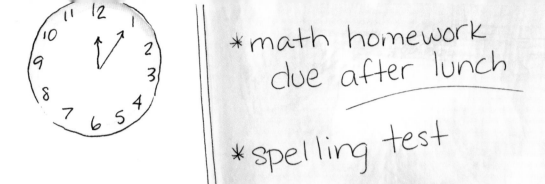

*math homework
due after lunch

* spelling test

There's so much more fun in a place filled with color,
Where all are **FREE** to enjoy one another.

THE END,
or maybe just the beginning of many more adventures...

Diverse City Discussion Points:

- If you were going to paint a picture of the outside - how many different colors would you need? (Blue sky, brown trees, green grass, etc.) Can you imagine going to art class and only having one color to use on your project? What would that be like?

- What about if you went to music class and the teacher only played one note, (bum, bum, bum, bum, bum, bum) over and over? Or if she played one song that was great but it was the only one you could ever listen to over and over - would that get boring?

- What about if you could only eat one kind of food for every meal and everything tasted the same? Do you know what spice is? (Salt, pepper, cinnamon) Spice adds flavor and makes food taste better. Different tastes add flavors to give us the variety that we enjoy.

- In this story, there were some kids being unkind to Jacob just because his skin color is different than their skin. How do you think that made him feel? Would you want to be left out of something just because your eyes were a different color than someone else? Or because your family was different than theirs? Or because you wore a (pick a color) shirt? I wouldn't like that - would you? We should always treat people the way we want to be treated.

- So, what should you do if you see someone being treated unfairly? It would be good for you to stand with your friend, like Zac did in the story and maybe even try to talk to the kids about it. Sometimes you just need to walk away and tell the teacher when someone is bullying another.

- Most importantly, let's celebrate and enjoy all of the colors, flavors, music, and variety of cultures in our world and help each other out. We are all different in one way or another and that is what makes each of us unique and valuable. There is a lot we can learn from each other when we are all free to be ourselves.

Tying these concepts into Martin Luther King Day and/or young author projects:

Dr. Martin Luther King, Jr. knew that it was wrong for people to be judged or treated unfairly because of the color of their skin. He was a leader who organized a march that created awareness and helped to bring about positive change so that all people would be treated equally. Dr. King had a dream that we would all be free. I hope that you will remember this story and help others as Dr. Martin Luther King did.

A note from Shawna Ray to young authors:

My son Zachary really does have a friend named Jacob, (See the boys' picture at the front of the book). The scene at recess really happened to Jacob and Zac, so this book is based on a true story. When Zac told me about what the kids said to Jacob I wished there was a way to help. I had never written a book before, but I woke up the next day with the idea to create a story where school kids go to an imaginary place called Diverse City (that part I made up). * The word Diversity means "the state of being diverse," which means, "difference and variety." When we take a trip, we expect and are open to new experiences, surroundings, and people that might be different than what we are use to. I want to always live in that state of mind. So, I wrote the book and had an editor review it and suggest changes. I had to write and rewrite it a lot before it all came together. My friend Laurie Faust is an amazing artist and I asked her to illustrate the book. She painted the pictures with water colors and scanned those images into the computer. It took almost two years to get everything together and find a publisher who would print the book.

You are all capable of taking your ideas and writing them out. It's important to keep reading, writing down your thoughts, listening to the advice of your teachers and parents, and rewriting things until they are done to the best of your ability. It's all part of the creative process, so don't give up. I look forward to reading your book someday!

"diversity." The American Heritage® Dictionary of the English Language, Fourth Edition. Houghton Mifflin Company, 2004. 28 Nov. 2006. Dictionary. www.dictionary.com

About the Author:

Shawna Ray is an author, singer, songwriter, and public speaker. Shawna graduated from Otterbein College in Westerville, Ohio with a Communications degree, specializing in Public Relations. She has worked for various non-profit organizations in the areas of Disability and Diversity Awareness Training, Development, and Community Relations. She lives in Columbus, Ohio with her son, Zachary, and daughter, Kaiya.
www.shawnaray.com

About the Illustrator:

Laurie Faust is a creative illustrator with numerous published children's books. She studied at Herron School of Art in Indianapolis, Indiana. Laurie has eighteen years of experience in graphic design and event design, which has opened doors to many other art and design opportunities including mural painting, invitation design, children's art, restaurant menu design, and themed artwork for restaurants. She lives in Noblesville, Indiana with her husband, Jeff, and their four children, Kiersten, Nick, and twins, Kathleen and Emily.
www.lauriefaustdesigns.com

About B5:

Atlanta, Georgia is home to the 5 dynamic brothers known as "B5"! You've seen them on Disney, Nickelodeon, MTV and BET; heard them on High School Musical, Hanna Montana and Disney! Growing up multi-racial, (black & white mix), the brothers have lived Diversity! "This is why we felt so passionate about participating with this project, because it all starts with the kids!" states Bryan. "Success, knowledge and love have no color! It's the way you think that makes the difference," says Patrick. "Diverse City" is 100% B5 Approved!! It lets kids know that we are all beautiful in our own way!
www.b5online.com